C000182193

The Little Black Dress

Megan Hess

The Little Black Dress

Hardie Grant

BOOKS

It is one of the true edicts of style that no matter the occasion, you can't go wrong with a little black dress.

A simple, well-cut black dress is the most versatile of all garments. It can take you from day to night, casual to formal and season to season with ease; nothing comes close for effortless sophistication. Whether you need to make an impression or blend in, feel comfortable or provoke a reaction, an LBD is always the answer. It's been said before but it's always true: a little black dress is the perfect foundation for any wardrobe.

Saint Laurent

Chanel

When Coco Chanel gave us the very first little black dress in 1926, her aim was to create a look that was truly accessible to all. In one bold move, the French couturier blew away the staid fashion of the day and replaced it with the careless abandon of the roaring twenties. A large part of the appeal was that Chanel's little black dress was ... well, little. Women everywhere celebrated the dress's relaxed structure and short hemline at a time when most gowns were floor length and restrictive. The press claimed it was the 'dress the whole world would wear'.

But perhaps most revolutionary part of Chanel's dress was the colour. Some say her use of black was an act of defiance against the uniform she wore as a child living in an orphanage. Others say it was a symbol of deep grief for her true love, Boy Capel, who was killed in a motorcycle accident in 1919. Others maintain she was making a statement about female independence, taking inspiration from maids and shopgirls who wore black while they worked. Whatever the cause, the colour became Coco's signature – and the very definition of chic.

Alexander
McQueen

Elie Saab

Countless designers have gone on to put their spin on the LBD, from Dior's feminine New Look to Givenchy's iconic gown for Audrey Hepburn in *Breakfast at Tiffany's* and Balenciaga's structurally delightful Envelope Dress – all original, black and fabulous. These dresses have been worn by some of the most influential women of the last decades: the biggest names of stage, screen and runway, and women who have literally made history. But the true beauty of the little black dress is that it is not just for top designers and celebrities. It is a look that everyone can embrace.

There have been era-defining LBDs in every decade of the last century. As fashion took a back seat during the Great Depression and World War II, many women relied on a single black dress that wouldn't show wear and tear and could be worn for many occasions. From there came the sophisticated coat dresses of the New Look in the 1940s, the mod shift dresses of the 1960s, the punk creations of the 1970s and 80s, and the minimalist sheaths of the 90s.

Lanvin

13

Céline

I remember vividly the day my mum bought me a black velvet cocktail dress by Australian designer Carla Zampatti for my high school formal. It was far more expensive than anything I'd ever owned, and I promised my mum it was a timeless classic that I'd wear forever. That dress still sits proudly in my wardrobe, having been dry-cleaned a million times. I've worn it to book launches, funerals and parties, special occasions and ordinary dinners. There are not many things that we can be sure of in life, but I can tell you that I will still be wearing that dress for as long as it fits. These days I spend so much of my time thinking about colour and love how working with a strict palette can evoke such a sense of elegance. In some ways, drawing a simple black dress is the most difficult because there is nowhere for the line work to hide.

For all its universal simplicity, the little black dress is a force to be reckoned with. It is a style that has persisted through the ages and given us some of the most memorable looks of all time. It has heralded revolutions, made stars into icons and marked eras. A little black dress has probably played a part in many of your own defining moments. While it may be ageless, timeless and classless, the LBD is far from boring. There is a story behind each and every one – including the beloved dresses in your own wardrobe.

Megan Hess

Giambattista Valli

17

Nothing is
more difficult
to make than a
little black dress.

Coco Chanel

—

The Ford Dress

by Chanel

—

1926

The woman who started it all. Chanel's original little black dress – a drop-hem, knee-length, full-sleeved cocktail dress in black crepe de chine – was nothing short of revolutionary. The daring simplicity, affordable fabric and relaxed structure broke away from the conservative fashions of the time and allowed women of all ages and means to be chic as well as comfortable. The press nicknamed Chanel's first little black dress the 'Ford Dress' after Henry Ford's car, which was equally accessible to all – and also only available in black.

31

NEL   CHANE

23

A black dress, flat pumps and a string of pearls – nothing could be more chic or more quintessentially Chanel.

Chanel

The Uniform

by Chanel

—

1959

Vogue predicted Chanel's little black dress would become 'a sort of uniform for all women of taste'. They were right. Chanel would evolve the concept in the following decades, introducing new cuts, fabrics and hemlines but never straying from her vision of an understated garment in the classic monochrome. Under Chanel's direction, black would cease to be the colour of menswear and mourning and instead become the colour of elegance.

I've been forty years discovering that the queen of all colours was *black.*

Pierre-Auguste Renoir

—

31

The New Look

by Dior

—

1947

Perhaps the opposite of Chanel's simple, understated frocks were the ultra-feminine silhouettes of Christian Dior's New Look in the 1940s and 50s. Dior was equally committed to the idea of a little black dress as a wardrobe staple – indeed he claimed every woman should have one. But his version, coming just two decades after the Ford Dress, was as luxurious and feminine as Chanel's was democratic and androgynous.

You can wear
black at any time.
You can wear
it at any age.
You may wear it for
almost any occasion;
a little black frock
is essential to a
woman's wardrobe.

Christian Dior

—

Dior

Despite his love of floral pinks and dove greys, Dior knew that when it came to style, black reigned supreme. 'I could write a book about black,' he mused in his *Little Dictionary of Fashion*.

With cinched waists, boned bodices and full skirts, Dior's little black dresses were designed to bring opulence and refinement back to French fashion after years of war and austerity. Sophia Loren was a picture of this New Look sophistication and elegance when she appeared in a black Dior gown on interview show *Person to Person* in 1958. Dior knew how to create a wardrobe for a rising star, and in doing so he cemented the little black dress in fashion history.

Sophia Loren

in Dior

—

1958

40

I love black
because it affirms,
designs and styles.
A woman in
a *black dress* is a
pencil stroke.

Yves Saint Laurent

—

Some of the most iconic little black dresses are from Hollywood's golden age. In the early years, film directors' love of a black dress was purely practical: when the technology for colour film was new, black could be relied upon not to distort, unlike other colours.

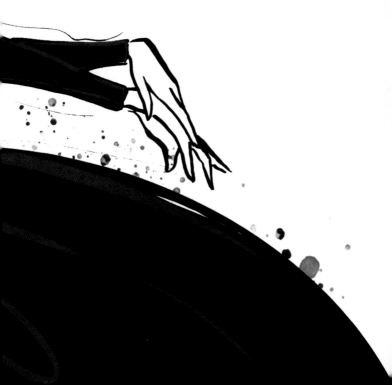

Rita Hayworth

in Jean Louis

Gilda

—

1946

This stunning, sensual black satin gown with matching elbow-length gloves was designed by Jean Louis, who once called it 'the most famous dress I ever made'. Louis was a costume designer for Columbia Pictures but had been given leave to work on *Gilda* for Universal Studios because of his relationship with Rita Hayworth. The star and designer collaborated on a dress for the ages – with a strapless bodice so that Hayworth could sing unimpeded, and an elaborate hidden harness and moulded plastic skirt to ensure it wouldn't move when she danced.

Grace Kelly

in Edith Head

Rear Window

—

1954

Edith Head was an absolute trailblazer, as the first woman in Hollywood to make it to lead costume designer. Grace Kelly in a pleated silk organza dress with translucent cap sleeves for *Rear Window* is one of Head's classic looks. Accessorised with a triple-strand pearl necklace and a bold red lip, it would have made Chanel herself proud.

A designer
is only as good
as the *star* who
wears her clothes.

Edith Head

—

Sophia Loren

in Edith Head

That Kind of Woman

—

1959

Sophia Loren's black peplum coat dress in *That Kind of Woman* was another Edith Head creation. The elegantly cinched waist and demure, refined cut was effortlessly sophisticated without detracting an ounce from Loren's signature va-va-voom. Head's work on so many classic films made her a taste maker almost without rival, and she knew how to deploy a little black dress to convey maximum on-screen glamour.

53

Elizabeth Taylor

in Oliver Messel

Suddenly Last Summer

—

1959

Oliver Messel created all of Elizabeth Taylor's looks in *Suddenly Last Summer,* and this chic black dress is a classic. With a slit neckline, short sleeves and cinched waist, it is the epitome of Hollywood glamour in the 1950s, and yet somehow it hasn't dated. Messel was a set designer first and foremost, but with this little black dress he more than proved his mettle in the realms of fashion.

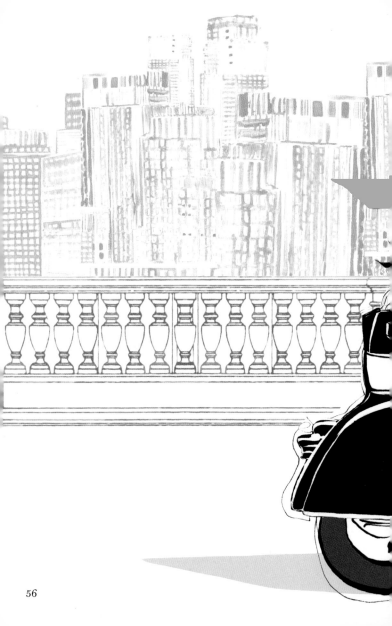

57

Elegance is the
only *beauty* that
never fades.

Audrey Hepburn

—

Audrey Hepburn

in Givenchy

Sabrina

—

1954

Audrey Hepburn's tea-length black dress from *Sabrina* is the thing fashion dreams are made of. The boat neck with bows on the shoulders was endlessly copied, immortalised as the 'Sabrina' neckline. The dress is also part of fashion folklore. Hepburn reportedly chose it herself from a selection of finished pieces in the atelier of then 26-year-old Hubert de Givenchy. The film won an Oscar for Best Costume Design – which Edith Head collected. Givenchy was never credited for the design.

Audrey Hepburn began
a lifelong friendship with
Givenchy and wore his
iconic black dresses both
on and off screen.

TIFFANY & CO.

GIVENCHY

63

Audrey Hepburn

in Givenchy

Breakfast at Tiffany's

—

1961

This famous friendship would lead to the creation of the most famous little black dress of all: the impossibly chic gown in the opening scenes of *Breakfast at Tiffany's*. By the time she was cast as Holly Golightly, Hepburn was an undisputed star who could demand to be dressed by whoever she chose. She chose Givenchy, who designed her a simple knee-length dress with a high neck and elegant cutaways at the shoulder blades. Edith Head reproduced the design for the film, lengthening the skirt to the ankle.

The *little black dress*
is the hardest thing
to realise, because
you must keep
it simple.

Hubert de Givenchy

—

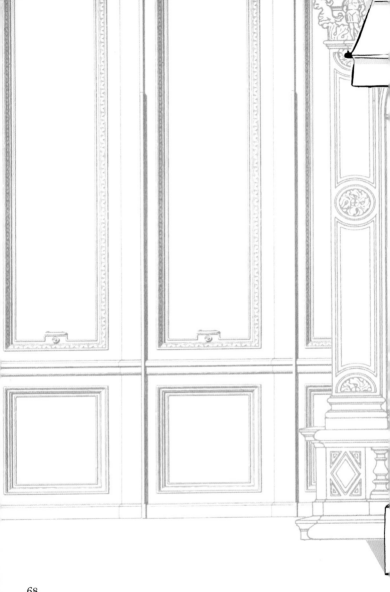

Café

Dior

Marilyn Monroe

The Asphalt Jungle

—

1950

Another legend of the silver screen, Marilyn Monroe is of course most remembered in that white pleated halter-neck dress, but she was just as captivating in black. When the young actress was on the cusp of stardom, she took a supporting role in *The Asphalt Jungle* and stole the show in this tight black dress with off-the-shoulder straps, perfectly paired with diamonds. Monroe would return to reliably chic black many times over her career.

71

Marilyn Monroe

in Dior

'The Last Sitting'

—

1962

Just six weeks before her death, Monroe sat for a now-famous *Vogue* shoot at the Hotel Bel-Air. 'The Last Sitting', as it would become known, took place over three champagne-fuelled days and resulted in some of the most candid photos of Monroe ever taken, including a sequence in a backless Dior gown with long sleeves and a full skirt. Shot in black-and-white, the images exude elegance and grace. The editors debated removing the feature entirely after Monroe's death, but chose instead to run it alongside a beautiful tribute penned by young staff writer Joan Didion.

Babs Simpson was the *Vogue* editor who dressed Monroe in that backless Dior gown. Simpson championed the minimal look long before it became fashionable; one of her assistants in the 1950s recalled her as wearing 'nothing but black dresses and huge jewels'.

Dior

Women who wear *black* lead colourful lives.

Neiman Marcus

—

You only have to look at a full orchestra in head-to-toe black to understand the power of monochrome on stage. The little black dress is a look that solo stars have harnessed time and time again.

Etta
James

—

Etta James cemented her personal style
early in her career with a sequinned
black halter dress and oversized
earrings. She was only a teenager at the
time but looked every bit the fierce soul
singer she would become. James later
said, 'My mother always told me, even
if a song has been done a thousand
times, you can still bring something of
your own to it.' The same can be said
for a little black dress.

83

Edith Piaf

on stage in Reims

—

1960

French singer Edith Piaf's signature look was a knee-length, long-sleeved black dress with a sweetheart neckline. She wore it whenever she performed. Some say the trademark look came about through necessity, because the struggling singer couldn't afford anything else. Piaf herself had a better explanation: 'I don't want my appearance to distract from the performance.'

When a
little black dress
is right, there is
nothing to wear
in its place.

Edith Piaf

—

Aretha Franklin

1970

Aretha Franklin knew how to
dress like a star, and her on-stage
outfits were as captivating as her
performances. The black gown she
wore on variety series *This Is Tom
Jones*, resplendent with diamante
detailing on the torso and paired with
a cape and head wrap, commanded
attention in all the right ways.

Whitney Houston

The Bodyguard

—

1992

Sometimes the job of the little black dress is to simply take a back seat, like the halter-style black gown Whitney Houston wore in *The Bodyguard*. What else to pair with a beaded Cleopatra head-dress and arm stacked with bracelets? With the outfit setting the scene, it was Houston's voice that ultimately stole the show.

91

Black is always elegant. It is the most complete colour in the whole world, made of all the colours in the palette.

Riccardo Tisci

—

The Envelope Dress

by Balenciaga

—

1961

Some little black dresses still become classics despite hardly being worn at all. Basque designer Cristóbal Balenciaga's trailblazing Envelope Dress, seen on the couture catwalk in 1961 and only ever sold to one or two clients, may not be the most practical garment to have in your wardrobe, but what it lacks in wearability it more than make up for in originality. The sculptural manipulation of fabric and totally new approach to design and structure make this dress utter black magic.

When colour is taken out of the equation, proportions, cut and texture must be executed perfectly – something master couturier Balenciaga knew all too well. It's no surprise to learn that Coco Chanel and Christian Dior were both fans, and Hubert de Givenchy was his student.

Balenciaga

99

The Rose Dress

by Balenciaga

Vogue

—

1967

The colour black dominated Balenciaga's work. *Harper's Bazaar* described his black as 'velvety, a night without stars, which makes the ordinary black seem almost gray'. Balenciaga took inspiration from traditional clergy robes, Spanish folk dress and Spain's Old Masters, and pushed the limits of what a simple black dress could be. In 1967 he used stiff silk gazar to create a caped gown that wrapped around the body like a rose. It is nothing short of divine.

Elegance is
elimination.

Cristóbal Balenciaga

—

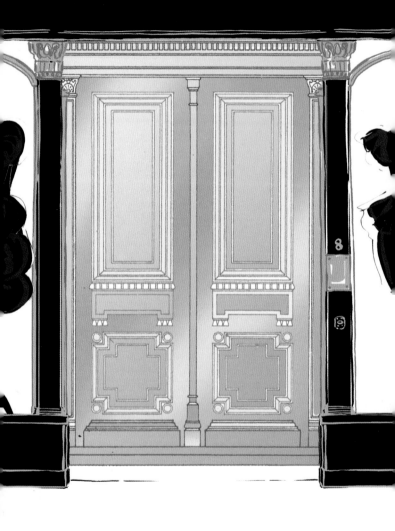

The LBD signified cultural shifts. As women became more independent in the 1960s, a little black dress accommodated newfound freedoms. And in the 1990s, the little black dress came into its own as the easiest way to embrace the modern minimalist look.

Giambattista Valli

Twiggy

1966

The face of 1966, model Twiggy put
the 'little' back into the little black
dress. The mod spin on the classic look
was an impossibly short shift dress
that sat high above the knee. Teamed
with Twiggy's pixie haircut, bold
eyeliner and boyish brogues, it was
an era-defining look.

Elizabeth Hurley

in Versace

Four Weddings and a Funeral premiere
—
1994

When Liz Hurley wore Gianni Versace's famous safety pin dress, she was a barely known actress. The revealing silk and lycra gown had debuted on the runway at Milan Fashion Week that year, worn by supermodel Helena Christensen. Versace made a last-minute decision to offer it to Hurley for this event, and it became one of the most famous red-carpet dresses of the 1990s. Versace's sister Donatella later said of the breakout look, 'Gianni made that dress for a woman who is sure of herself and who isn't afraid to break the rules. Liz embodied all of this in an extraordinary way.'

The *little black dress*
expresses a moment
of freedom and
individuality
every time.

André Leon Talley

—

Princess Diana

in Christina Stambolian

'The Revenge Dress'

—

1994

This off-the-shoulder chiffon cocktail dress by Greek designer Christina Stambolian had languished at the back of Princess Diana's wardrobe for years, deemed 'unroyal' by those who thought a princess should be demure and reserved. But in 1994, as Charles's indiscretions came to light, Diana made a hasty but strategic decision – swapping out the gown she had planned to wear to the Serpentine Gallery annual party and instead stepping out in the statement little black dress. She looked every part the modern woman, totally in command of her own image, and blew the entire world away.

A little black dress worn by a powerful woman can be either a bold statement or an act of quiet diplomacy – such is the versatility of the style.

Elie Saab

119

Jackie
Onassis

—

1960s

The original White House style icon,
Jacqueline Kennedy Onassis inspired
so many women with her sleek, elegant
fashion. She was a masterful wearer
of accessories and knew that there is
no better backdrop for pearls and silk
scarves than a well-cut black dress.

I want people to see
the *dress* but focus
on the woman.

Vera Wang

—

Michelle Obama

in Vera Wang

White House State Dinner

—

2015

Another White House resident who knew the versatility of a black dress was Michelle Obama. She chose the classic colour for many of her public appearances as First Lady. The custom-made Vera Wang gown she wore to a state dinner in 2015 was a stunning example, its mermaid silhouette and off-the-shoulder neckline reminiscent of Old Hollywood glamour.

Simplicity is
the ultimate
sophistication.

Leonardo da Vinci

—

A century after the little black dress was first championed by Chanel, it shows no signs of going anywhere. Designers revamp the look with each season, but it is the classics that have really stood the test of time.

Marion Cotillard

in Dior

—

2012

In 2012, French actress Marion Cotillard was photographed in a number of original Dior dresses for the first issue of their house magazine. To see her in this New Look–inspired black dress is to understand that this style truly is timeless.

Dior

The New LBD

by Chanel

Look 86, Pre-Fall

—

2018

Chanel's designers have maintained the little black dress as a house code. Karl Lagerfeld's 2018 Pre-Fall collection was almost entirely black and included a monochrome dress with dropped hem and long sleeves reminiscent of the Ford Dress. After all the iterations of that iconic look that have graced the runway, the inimitable couturier was surely reminding us that the original has never really gone out of style.

One is never
overdressed or
underdressed
with a
little black dress.

Karl Lagerfeld

—

139

Thank you.

To Emily Hart and Arwen Summers for creating another wonderful fashion book together. To Martina Granolic for diving head-first into every single little black dress ever created and finding the absolute gems. To Andrea Davison for so beautifully researching every single hidden detail. To Murray Batten for creating such a chic and elegant design on our ninth book together! To Todd Rechner for your incredible care and perfection in seeing my books to their finished form. To Justine Clay for first discovering my work and setting me on my way. To my husband Craig and my children Gwyn and Will for being my biggest inspiration.

Miu Miu

141

Megan Hess was destined to draw.

After working in graphic design and art direction, Megan illustrated Candace Bushnell's bestselling book *Sex and the City* in 2008. Her career in fashion illustration has since seen her creating for renowned clients all over the world, including portraits for *Vanity Fair*, animations for Prada in Milan, the windows of Bergdorf Goodman in New York, and live illustrating for fashion shows such as Christian Dior Couture. Megan is the author of nine bestselling fashion books and the sensational *Claris: The Chicest Mouse in Paris* series.

Visit Megan at meganhess.com

Published in 2022 by Hardie Grant Books, an imprint of Hardie Grant Publishing

Hardie Grant Books (Melbourne)
Wurundjeri Country
Building 1, 658 Church Street
Richmond, Victoria 3121

Hardie Grant Books (London)
5th & 6th Floors
52–54 Southwark Street
London SE1 1UN

hardiegrantbooks.com

A catalogue record for this book is available from the National Library of Australia

Megan Hess: The Little Black Dress
ISBN 978 1 74379 735 8

10 9 8 7 6 5 4 3 2 1

Publisher: Arwen Summers
Project Editor: Emily Hart
Researcher: Andrea Davison
Design Manager: Kristin Thomas
Designer: Murray Batten
Production Manager: Todd Rechner
Production Coordinator: Jessica Harvie

Colour reproduction by Splitting Image Colour Studio
Printed in China by Leo Paper Products LTD.

The paper this book is printed on is from FSC®-certified forests and other sources. FSC® promotes environmentally responsible, socially beneficial and economically viable management of the world's forests.

Hardie Grant acknowledges the Traditional Owners of the country on which we work, the Wurundjeri people of the Kulin nation and the Gadigal people of the Eora nation, and recognises their continuing connection to the land, waters and culture. We pay our respects to their Elders past, present and emerging.

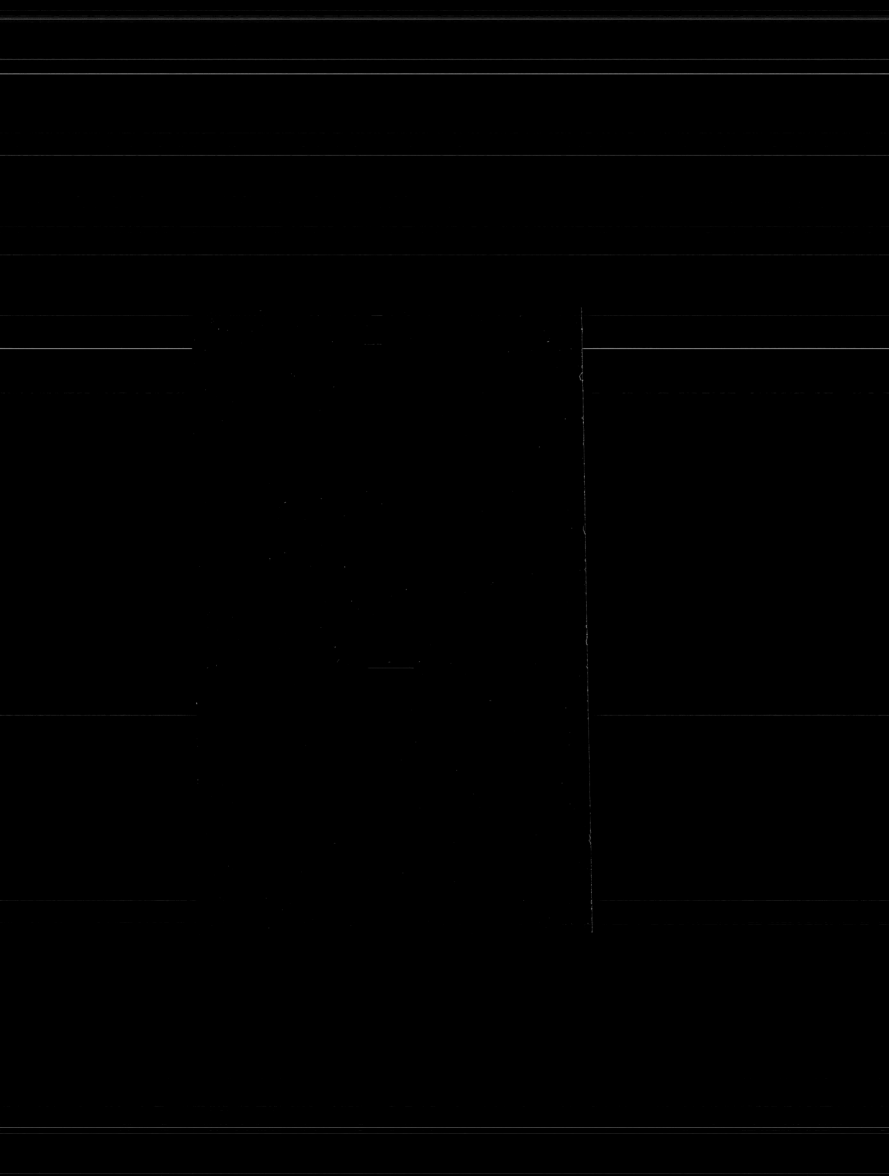